Slim Goodbody's
LIGHTEN UP
SERIES

THE SHAPE OF GOOD NUTRITION:
THE FOOD PYRAMID

Crabtree Publishing Company
www.crabtreebooks.com

Series Development and Packaging: John Burstein, Slim Goodbody Corp.
Senior Script Development: Phoebe Backler
Managing Editor: Valerie J. Weber
Designer and Illustrator: Ben McGinnis
Graphic Design Agency: Adventure Advertising
Instructional Designer: Alan Backler, Ph. D.
Content Consultant: Betty Hubbard, Ed. D., Certified Health Education Specialist
Project Editor: Reagan Miller

Library and Archives Canada Cataloguing in Publication

Burstein, John.
        The shape of good nutrition : the food pyramid / Slim
Goodbody.

(Slim Goodbody's lighten up!)
ISBN 978-0-7787-3918-0 (bound).--ISBN 978-0-7787-3937-1 (pbk.)

        1. Nutrition--Juvenile literature.   2. Food--Juvenile literature.
I. Title.   II. Series: Goodbody, Slim.   Slim Goodbody's lighten up!
TX355.G63 2008   j613.2
C2008-900731-X

Library of Congress Cataloging-in-Publication Data

Burstein, John.
        The shape of good nutrition : the food pyramid / John Burstein.
            p. cm. -- (Slim goodbody's lighten up!)
        Includes index.
        ISBN-13: 978-0-7787-3919-7 (rlb)
        ISBN-10: 0-7787-3919-8 (rlb)
        ISBN-13: 978-0-7787-3937-1 (pb)
        ISBN-10: 0-7787-3937-6 (pb)
        1. Nutrition--Juvenile literature. I. Title. II. Series.

RA784.B79 2008
613.2--dc22
                                                                2008003596

Crabtree Publishing Company

www.crabtreebooks.com   1-800-387-7650

Published in Canada
Crabtree Publishing
616 Welland Ave.
St. Catharines, Ontario
L2M 5V6

Published in the United States
Crabtree Publishing
PMB16A
350 Fifth Ave., Suite 3308
New York, NY 10118

Published in the United Kingdom
Crabtree Publishing
White Cross Mills
High Town, Lancaster
LA1 4XS

Published in Australia
Crabtree Publishing
386 Mt. Alexander Rd.
Ascot Vale (Melbourne)
VIC 3032

Printed in the U.S.A.

TABLE OF CONTENTS

Slim Goodbody's
LIGHTEN UP
SERIES

HELLO THERE. I'M SLIM GOODBODY,

and my greatest goal in life is to help young people across the planet become healthy and active. After all, one in three kids in the United States is overweight. Without changing their eating and exercise habits, many of these young people will become overweight adults. They risk many possible health problems like **high blood pressure** or **diabetes**. I am here today to introduce you to my friend Simon. This summer, Simon is working as an assistant cook at Whispering Pines Camp. Join him as he learns about **nutrition**, eating well, and living a healthy lifestyle.

Know Your Nutrients

Hi! My name is Simon. I love cooking healthy, delicious food. Someday, I hope to be the head chef at my own restaurant. First, however, I need to learn more about working in a kitchen. This summer, I decided to get a job as an assistant cook at Whispering Pines Camp.

A week before camp started, my friend Ben came over. He planned to work at Whispering Pines Camp, too, as the head tennis coach.

"I can't believe you're going to be the cook at camp," said Ben, shaking his head. "You're going to be inside all summer long, and you won't be able to teach the campers anything back in the kitchen."

A Winning Strategy

"I know it probably sounds crazy to you, but I love to cook. If I do my job well and feed the kids healthy food, they'll have way more energy and they'll grow strong. Your tennis players will be able to thank ME if they win their tennis matches!" I laughed.

"Oh, really!?" said Ben, smiling. "I'm not so sure about that."

"I still have a lot to learn about nutrition, though. Do you want to help me?" I asked.

"Why not?" said Ben, shrugging his shoulders.

As I turned on my computer, I remembered my health teacher's advice. She told me that web sites with addresses ending in *.gov* and *.edu* are created by the government and schools. These groups are not trying to sell you something, so you can trust their information. It's reliable and **valid**.

.GOV
.EDU

THE ROLE OF NUTRIENTS

The first web site we found explained that food is made up of different chemicals called **nutrients**. All together there are six different kinds of nutrients. Each one has its own job. The web site also explained that you need all six nutrients to stay healthy, grow strong, and have a lot of energy.

Carbohydrates are your body's main source of energy.

Proteins are used to build and repair your cells.

Minerals are used to keep your teeth and bones strong. They also help your body absorb other nutrients in the food.

Vitamins are needed to keep your eyes and skin healthy and help protect you against **infections**.

Fats are a power-packed, concentrated energy source.

Water helps move nutrients through every cell of your body.

"But how do you know you're eating enough of each nutrient? You don't walk into a restaurant and order a nice hot carbohydrate with some vitamins on the side!" said Ben with a chuckle.

"Good point!" I laughed.

Carbohydrates
Proteins
Minerals
Vitamins   Fats
Water

5

THE FOOD PYRAMID: BUILDING A HEALTHY MEAL

I kept surfing the Internet until I found a colorful diagram called the "food pyramid." "It says here that if you follow the food pyramid suggestions, you'll get all of the nutrients that you need," I said. "Here's the way it works. The food pyramid has a stripe for each of the five major food groups (grains, fruits, vegetables, milk, and meats and beans) and a stripe for oils."

"Why aren't all of the stripes the same size?" asked Ben.

"You're supposed to eat more from the food groups with the wider stripes and less from the groups with the narrower stripes," I explained. "The meat and beans food group is important because you get minerals and proteins from eating meat. But meat also has a lot of fat and **cholesterol**. If you eat too much of it, you can suffer from high cholesterol and heart problems. That's why the meat and beans food group stripe is narrower."

GRAINS
Make half of your grains whole.

VEGETABLES
Vary your veggies

FRUITS
Focus on fruits.

MILK
Get your calcium-rich foods.

MEAT & BEANS
Go lean with protein.

OILS
Oils are not a food group, but you need some for good health. Get your oils from fish, nuts, and liquid oils such as corn oil, soybean oil, and canola oil.

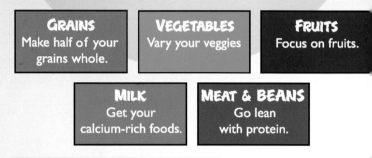

A CHANGE IN SIZE

"See how each stripe is wider at the bottom and skinnier at the top?" I went on. "That's because there's healthy and unhealthy foods in all of the groups. If you look at the vegetable stripe, the high-fat, unhealthy vegetables like French fries are in the skinny section at the top. The **nutritious**, low-fat vegetables like baked sweet potatoes are in the wide section at the bottom."

"So you're supposed to eat more of the foods in the wide part at the bottom of each food group stripe," observed Ben.

"Right. And the little dude climbing up the side of the pyramid is supposed to remind you that exercising every day is really important, too."

COACHING VERSUS COOKING

"OK, Mr. Nutrition. But I still say that my tennis players will win their matches because I am a great coach!" said Ben with a smirk.

"All right," I said, smiling. "Let's make a bet. I bet that the campers will be better athletes this summer because of my cooking."

"I bet they'll be better because of my coaching!" said Ben laughing.

Slim Goodbody Says: People of different cultures eat different kinds of foods. Eating a balanced meal is important no matter what culture you are from.

USE YOUR BRAIN, EAT WHOLE GRAIN

The next week, I arrived at the Whispering Pines Camp kitchen, ready to work. The head cook Harold was already in the kitchen, preparing lunch for the campers.

"Well, hello, Simon!" Harold said with a big grin. "I'm just getting started with lunch. Come on in and give me a hand choosing a grain for the kids."

"Great," I replied. "I've been learning a lot about healthy grains and the food pyramid."

"Fantastic. Like what?" asked Harold.

Grains are a good source of vitamins and minerals, too!

GREAT GRAINS, FABULOUS FIBER

"Well, one thing that I remember is that grains are a good source of carbohydrates, our bodies main energy source. They also have **fiber**, which helps us **digest** food," I said.

"You bet. And what kinds of foods are considered grains?" asked Harold.

"Well, grains like wheat, rice, and oats are in this group, and so are foods made out of grains like cereal, bread, and pasta," I explained.

"I guess you know a thing or two about food!" said Harold.

Slim Goodbody Says: Bagels, fry bread, and wanton wrappers are just a few examples of grains that are eaten in different cultures around the world.

WHAT MAKES A WHOLE GRAIN WHOLE?

"We need to choose a grain for our lunch today. What do you think about using a whole grain?" Harold asked.

"To be honest, I can never remember what whole grains are," I admitted.

"No problem. I'd be surprised if you knew everything on the first day!" said Harold with a grin. "Brown rice, whole cornmeal, oatmeal, and bulgur are all examples of whole grains. Whole grains are healthier than **refined** grains like white rice or white bread are, because they contain more nutrients and fiber."

Slim Goodbody Says: Whole grains have all three parts of a grain — the bran, the endosperm, and the germ.

WHOLE GRAIN

Bran
Endosperm
Germ

"So what kinds of whole grains can we choose from?" I asked.

"Well, let's see. We have some bagels here," said Harold, looking at the ingredients list on the back of the package. "Sure enough! These bagels are made with whole-wheat flour."

"Great! Let's use those!"

"In the future, we can also pop popcorn, add some brown rice to a soup, or make oatmeal cookies for dessert! Those are all whole grains that the campers will love!" added Harold

THE VALUE OF VEGETABLES

Once the bagels were unwrapped and ready to be served, we moved on to preparing vegetables for the campers.

"OK, Simon. What kind of vegetable would you like to prepare for the kids today? We can serve raw broccoli, steamed carrots, canned peas, or frozen corn. We also have 100-percent vegetable juice," said Harold.

A VARIETY OF VEGETABLES

"Those all sound good," I said. "Do you ever experiment with vegetables from other cultures, too?"

"You bet," answered Harold. "I like cooking with anything, from Asian bamboo shoots and bok choy to South American chilies. I also have a great recipe for Louisiana okra. I love experimenting with different vegetables. They're good for you, and they add new and interesting flavors to meals. But I think that we should serve raw broccoli spears for lunch today."

"Broccoli is a great choice," I said. "I learned in health class that dark green and orange vegetables are the healthiest ones because they have many nutrients."

Slim Goodbody Says: All vegetables are full of vitamins, minerals, carbohydrates, and fiber. Some examples of dark-green vegetables include broccoli, collard greens, romaine lettuce, and spinach. Did you know that most dark-green vegetables are a good source of minerals like calcium and iron?

Orange vegetables include butternut squash, carrots, and sweet potatoes. Most orange vegetables contain vitamin A, which keeps your eyes and skin healthy and helps protect against infections.

"Yes, indeed. Unfortunately, most people don't eat enough vegetables," said Harold.

"I know, but I just don't get it. There are so many delicious vegetables. Adding frozen chopped spinach, collard greens, or kale to a pot of soup is always tasty. Raw carrot sticks and red pepper strips make a great snack, too," I said.

A Salty Snack

Just then, Ben poked his head into the kitchen.

"Hey, guys. My tennis players are getting hungry. Do you have any snacks that I can bring out to them? A bag of potato chips would be great," said Ben.

"Potato chips have too much oil and salt, right, Harold?" I looked to Harold for advice.

OILS CAN SPOIL

"It's important to get some oil in your diet. Some foods, like avocados, nuts, and salmon, actually contain oils that are good for you," explained Harold. "In general, though, it makes sense to choose foods that are made without oils. Why don't you take some apples to your campers? That snack should help them make it through until lunch time."

"Thanks! Apples will be great," said Ben, waving goodbye.

When he was gone, I turned back to Harold. "What kinds of oil do you use for cooking?" I asked.

"Well, I try to use olive oil, corn oil, or canola oil. They are the healthiest oils that you can use for cooking. Unfortunately, many people eat food that's made with **hydrogenated** oils."

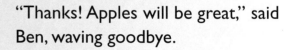

Slim Goodbody Says: The number-one killer in North America is coronary heart disease. The **arteries** to the heart become clogged and narrowed, and not enough blood can get through to the heart. Without enough blood, the heart lacks the oxygen and nutrients that it needs to work well. High blood pressure makes the heart work harder to pump blood to the body. Stay away from salty snacks and oily foods to keep your heart healthy.

HYDRO WHAT?

"Hydrogenated oils?" I asked, looking confused.

"Lard, shortening, margarine, and butter are all hydrogenated oils. They're often made from the fat of cows, chickens, and pigs. Some kinds are made from vegetables, too," explained Harold.

"When they're at room temperature, hydrogenated oils are solid. The healthier oils, like olive oil, stay liquid when they get cool," he added. "Hydrogenated oils are very unhealthy. If you eat too much food that's made with hydrogenated oil, it can lead to all sorts of health issues."

"So what's the best way to avoid foods with oils?" I asked.

"The best thing to do is to take a look at the ingredients list on a package of any food. See if hydrogenated oils are in the ingredients list, and you'll know if the food is healthy or not," said Harold reassuringly.

HYDROGENATED OILS

LARD

SHORTENING

MARGARINE

BUTTER

SUBSTITUTES FOR OILS

"Let's try not to use unhealthy oils in our meals this summer. We can find baking recipes that use vegetable oil instead of butter or shortening. We can also make our salad dressings with olive oil and vinegar," I suggested.

"We should also make sure that the campers get enough healthy oils from avocados and nuts," added Harold.

Slim Goodbody Says: Can you think of other ways to use healthy oils in your meals? When you are choosing a snack, remember to look at the ingredients list for the word *hydrogenated*. If you see that word, try to find a different snack!

FRUITS MAKE YOU FEEL FANTASTIC

While I cut up the broccoli into spears for lunch, I asked, "What kind of fruit should we serve for lunch?"

"Well, we've got frozen berries, dried apples, or fresh pineapple. We also have 100-percent grapefruit juice."

Slim Goodbody Says: Fruits have many important nutrients, including vitamins, minerals, carbohydrates, and fiber. For example, many different fruits contain vitamin C. Did you know that vitamin C helps your body repair damaged **tissue** and helps you grow? It also helps heal cuts and wounds and keeps your teeth and gums healthy!

Which of these fruits are high in vitamin C?

lemons
oranges
apples
blueberries

Answer: All of them!

"Those all sound good. Do you ever serve fruits from different parts of the world?" I asked. "Kumquats, star fruits, and papayas are so delicious!"

"That's a great idea," said Harold. "We'll have to order some."

kumquat

star fruit

Kumquats were originally grown in China and throughout Asia.
Star fruits first appeared in Sri Lanka and Indonesia but have been grown across Southeast Asia and Malaysia for hundreds of years.
Papayas are native to southern Mexico and Central America.

papaya

COLOR US HEALTHY

"My health teacher told us to eat different kinds and colors of fruit to make sure that we get the vitamins and minerals that we need. She tried to get us to think of five fruits that are all different colors," I said.

"Wow, that sounds tough," laughed Harold. "How about red strawberries, purple grapes, orange mangos, green kiwis, and brown figs?" "There's also pink grapefruit juice and yellow bananas," I added.

Slim Goodbody Says: Be careful when you choose fruit at the store. Canned fruit often comes in sugary syrup that is high in **calories** and low in nutrients. Many fruit juices are made with extra sugar, too. Look for the words "100% fruit juice" on the label to make sure that you get the best canned fruit.

"All right," said Harold, "what fruit are we going to give the campers today?"

"Let's serve the fresh pineapple. We can also make sure that there's a bowl of fresh fruit on the table all the time so that the kids can snack on it," I suggested.

Slim Goodbody Says: How can you eat more fruit in your diet? Bring a banana to school with you for a snack. Eat apples and peanut butter if you are hungry when you get home from school.

WHAT'S SO COOL ABOUT CALCIUM?

"OK, Simon. So far, we're planning to serve bagels, raw broccoli spears, and fresh pineapple, and we're going to avoid unhealthy oils. We need to offer something from the milk food group today, too," reflected Harold.

"Well, what are our options?" I asked.

"We can put a slice of cheddar cheese on the bagels, have yogurt on the side, or serve a glass of milk," answered Harold.

LOW-FAT VERSUS FULL-FAT FOODS

"We can't go wrong with any of those choices," I said. "What about serving ice cream for dessert?"

Slim Goodbody Says: Milk products are full of important vitamins and minerals. They contain calcium and potassium, minerals that are good for building and strengthening healthy muscles, bones, and teeth. Vitamin D is added to most milk because it allows the body to absorb calcium.

"I like using low-fat milk products like skim milk and low-fat yogurt. Ice cream and whole milk have calcium, too, but they're fattening. I want our campers to be healthy and fit by the end of this summer," said Harold.

"Then why don't we serve low-fat yogurt today?" I suggested.

Slim Goodbody Says: Did you know that some foods that are made from milk, such as cream cheese, cream, and butter, are not considered part of the milk food group? That is because in the process of making these different kinds of food, they lose their calcium!

"That sounds great. In the future, we can make oatmeal, hot chocolate, or tomato soup with milk instead of water to make sure that the kids get enough calcium. Fat-free yogurt on baked potatoes or as a dip for vegetables is good, too," said Harold, rubbing his stomach.

Slim Goodbody Says: People who are lactose intolerant can't digest a chemical in milk that's called lactose. They feel sick if they eat most milk products. Of course, they still need calcium, so they have to eat foods without lactose, such as yogurt or special lactose-free milk. They can also get calcium from some kinds of juice, cereal, breads, and leafy, green vegetables, such as kale, spinach, and collard greens. Some kinds of canned fish and dried beans have calcium, too.

PROTEIN POWER

"Well, Harold," I said, "We still need something from the meat and beans food group. We've got to make sure that the campers get enough protein to build their muscles and bones."

"Protein also helps you keep your **cartilage**, blood, and skin healthy. But the meat and beans food group gives us a lot more than protein. It provides us with zinc, iron, B vitamins, magnesium, and vitamin E, too. Of course, most people don't get all of those vitamins and minerals," said Harold, shaking his head. "Most people only eat chicken, turkey, pork, and beef from the meat food group. They don't realize what they're missing! Fish, dried beans, peas, eggs, nuts, and seeds are all in the meat food group, too."

"I get your point, Harold, but we don't have time to prepare all of the different foods in the meat and bean food group. What should we serve for lunch?" I asked.

ZINC
IRON

B VITAMINS
MAGNESIUM
VITAMIN E

Slim Goodbody Says: Get all of the nutrients and less of the fat. Before you cook red meat and poultry, cut off the skin and fat. Your meal will taste better, and it will be healthier for you.

FOODS FROM FAR AWAY

"If we want to be adventurous, we could offer Middle Eastern **falafel** and **hummus** or Southern catfish with black-eyed peas! They have all sorts of protein in them!" laughed Harold with a twinkle in his eyes.

"We could, but I think sliced turkey would taste better on a bagel sandwich!" I chuckled.

"That sounds good. Let's keep the campers healthy and vary their choices of foods from the meat and beans food group. We can put sunflower seeds in our salads and kidney beans in our vegetable soups. The campers love pea soup on a rainy day," said Harold.

"We could also add nuts and seeds to our cookies and muffins," I suggested.

THE PROOF IS IN THE GAME

Just as we were finishing making the last bagel sandwich, the giant bell rang outside, telling campers that it was time to eat. Within minutes, they were sitting down at their tables and gobbling up our meal.

That afternoon, Ben found us in the kitchen. "I have to hand it to you guys. My tennis players were fading away before lunch, but after they ate your meal, they were unstoppable," he said in disbelief.

"That's great, Ben," I said, feeling proud. "Does that mean that I won the bet?"

"First you have to help us win the end of the summer tournament against our rivals at Camp Silverbrook!" said Ben smiling.

"You're on!" I laughed.

HOW MUCH IS ENOUGH?

Later that day, we started working on our menu for the rest of the week. I soon realized that I still had a lot to learn.

"How much is each person supposed to eat?" I asked.

"Well, first you need to consider a person's age, **gender**, and the amount of exercise that he or she gets," explained Harold. "Our campers are between the ages of nine and thirteen. They exercise every day."

Harold then pulled out a poster.

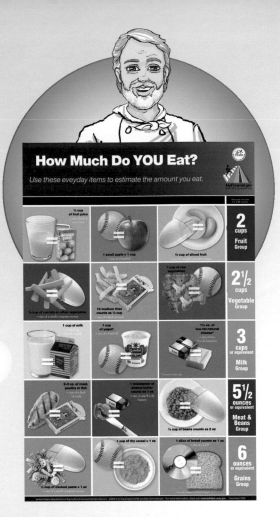

SERVING SIZE

BASEBALLS AND DOMINOES

"This chart shows that our boys should eat 2 cups (500ml) of fruit every day. This amount is about the size of two baseballs. Our girls should eat about 1 1/2 cups (375ml) worth of fruit every day," explained Harold. "As for vegetables, our campers need 2 1/2 cups (625ml) of vegetables every day."

"So they should eat 2 1/2 baseballs worth of green beans or carrots," I said.

"Right. They also need 3 cups (750ml) from the milk group every day," explained Harold. "If they wanted, they could eat 1 ounce (43g) of cheese or a piece the size of three dominoes instead. That amount would substitute for 1 cup (250ml) of milk," said Harold.

20

"What about the meat and bean food group?" I asked.

"Well, every day girls should eat 5 ounces (142g) of meat or beans, and boys should eat 5 1/2 ounces (156g). That amount of meat or beans looks the same size as two decks of playing cards," Harold explained.

"Of course, beans are an important part of the meat food group, too. Two ounces (57g) of meat is the same as 125ml of beans, or a serving the size of a computer mouse," said Harold. "Both boys and girls

should get 6 ounces (170g) of grains each day, too. A slice of bread weighs one ounce (28g), and so does a cup of cereal."

"Wow, I eat way more meat than I am supposed to. I'm pretty sure that I am not getting enough vegetables, too" I said. "Do you think that the campers know about these serving sizes?" I asked.

"I doubt it," said Harold. "Do you think you'd like to teach them?"

"You bet," I said. "I'm going to start a nutrition club for the campers."

Slim Goodbody Says: To see if you eat a healthy, balanced diet, make a list of everything that you eat today. At the end of the day, use the "How Much Do You Eat?" poster to see if you have eaten the right amount from each food group. If not, look on the next page for tips on how to make healthier choices.

HEALTHY CHOICES FOR A HEALTHY LIFE

By the second week of camp, my nutrition club was underway. We had talked about the six different nutrients in food and learned about the six stripes of the food pyramid. We even explored serving sizes and the "How Much Do You Eat?" poster. It was time to teach the kids the important skill of making healthy decisions. The campers sat in a circle and listened carefully.

"We all know that it can be tough to make healthy choices, right?" I started. "Eating that bowl of ice cream while you're watching TV seems a lot more appealing than munching on carrot sticks. But you can decide what would be better for you."

STEPPING TO A DECISION

"Today, I'm going to teach you an easy way to make good decisions. It's a simple process. The first step is to *identify your choices*. Then, you *evaluate each choice* and think about their consequences. Then, you *identify the healthiest decision*, and you *take action*. Finally, you *evaluate your decision* and decide if you should make the same choice in the future," I explained.

"Let's put this process to the test. Come with me into the kitchen." The campers followed me and watched as I opened the cupboard. "Your first step is to *identify your choices*, right? All right, gang, here are your choices. You can either have a doughnut or a piece of whole-wheat toast for a snack. Now you need to *evaluate your choices*. What do you already know about doughnuts and whole-wheat bread?"

WHOLE-WHEAT TOAST VERSUS THE DONUT

A camper raised his hand and said, "Whole-wheat bread is healthier because it's made with whole grains. Doughnuts are full of fat and sugar. They might taste good, but after you eat them, you feel gross."

"Well done," I said. "Now you can *identify the healthiest decision*."

"The whole-wheat toast is healthier so we should eat it," suggested another camper.

"OK! The next step is to *take action* and make your toast." After we'd eaten our snack, I explained, "The final step is to *evaluate your choice*. What did you think about the whole-wheat toast?"

"It tasted really good, and I feel great. I would definitely make that choice again," said one of the campers. The others agreed.

"So you see, making healthy choices can be a simple process. If you pay attention to what you eat, you can make healthy decisions every day," I said.

23

GREAT GOALS

As the summer continued, the kids in the nutrition club were eating well and exercising. They were all looking more fit and healthy. At one of our meetings, one of the girls said, "I feel so great. I have way more energy these days, and my skin and hair look better than ever. I didn't realize what a difference healthy food could make."

"Me neither," said one of the boys. "I'm just worried that I won't be able to keep eating well when I get home." The other campers agreed.

"It sounds like it's time to set some goals," I said handing each of them a piece of paper. "First, *write down a realistic goal*. Next, *list the steps that you need to take to reach your goal*. Then, *ask your friends and family for support in reaching your goal*. Then, *evaluate your progress and decide if you have reached your goal or not*. If you have, go ahead and *reward yourself!*" I explained. "Does anyone have an idea for a goal?"

SWIM-TEAM SUCCESS

"I do!" said one of the boys. "I've been getting better at swimming this summer. When I get back to school, I want to try out for the swim team."

"That's a fantastic goal! What steps will you need to take to make the team?" I asked.

"Well, I need to keep eating well. That way, I'll have the energy that I need to do my best. I'll need to find a pool where I can practice, too," he said.

"Will you need support from your friends and family?" I asked.

"I am going to ask my mom to help me eat well. If she buys healthy food at the store, I won't be as tempted to eat junk food," he said. "I can ask my friend to try out too. Maybe we can swim together. It's always more fun to exercise with a friend."

"Great," I said. "And how will you evaluate your progress?"

"I guess I'll know if I succeeded if I make the team!" he said.

"And how will you reward yourself if you do?" I asked.

"Hmm. I think I'll buy myself some new swimming goggles if I make the team," he said happily.

Slim Goodbody Says: Now it's your turn to make some goals. Use Simon's steps to make a goal for yourself about healthy eating.

- Set a realistic goal and write it down
- List the steps to reach the goal
- Get help/support from others
- Evaluate your progress
- Reward yourself with something healthy and fun

Spread the Word: Be a Health Advocate

As the summer came to an end, I decided to give my nutrition club one last challenge. "I am so proud of all of you. You've learned so much about nutrition and eating well this summer. I think that you're all ready to be health advocates," I said.

"What's a health advocate?" asked the campers.

"A health advocate is someone who encourages others to make good choices and to work toward a healthy lifestyle. We need more health advocates in our world to keep our families and communities healthy and strong," I told them. "Let me describe what a health advocate does."

I'M A HEALTH ADVOCATE!

HOW TO BE A SUCCESSFUL HEALTH ADVOCATE

"The first step is to *take a healthy stand on an issue.* Then, you *persuade others to make a healthy choice.* Finally, you have to *be convincing!*" I explained. "Do any of you have ideas for how you can be health advocates when you get back home?"

"I do," said one of the girls. "My family eats so much fast food, and they never exercise. I've already decided that when I get back home, I'm going to try to help them get healthy."

"Wow, that's great. How will you persuade your family to eat healthier food?

"I'm going to offer to help my parents go grocery shopping and cook dinner. I can use your recipes to show them that healthy food can taste really good."

"Do you think that you can be convincing?" I asked.

"Are you kidding? Once they see how good I look, they will want to know all of my tricks! I can tell them from experience that if they pay attention and work hard, they will be able to look great and feel good, too. I can also help them understand the health problems that they could have if they don't make healthier choices."

Slim Goodbody Says: Now it's your turn. Use these three steps to become a health advocate:
• Take a healthy stand on an issue
• Persuade others to make a healthy choice
• Be convincing
You could work with your friends to get healthier food in the cafeteria. Help your parents plan meals and choose healthier foods at the grocery store. Design a poster about making healthy choices and put it up in your school hallway. Remember, you can help make your family and community strong and healthy, too.

SIMON SUMS UP THE SUMMER

On the last day of camp, I found Harold in the kitchen.

"I can't believe the summer is over," I said, shaking my head.

"Time flies when you're having fun!" said Harold with a grin.

"You can say that again," I nodded.

"Have you spent any time thinking about what you learned this summer?" asked Harold.

"I've learned a ton, thanks to you and the campers. The food pyramid and the 'How Much Do You Eat' poster have helped me make sure that I eat the right amount of food from the different food groups. I can tell that I'm getting the nutrients I need. I think that all of this healthy food is helping me be smarter!

"I've been exercising, too," I told Harold, "and I feel stronger and more energetic than ever. I know the campers do, too. It's amazing what a difference it makes to eat from all of the food groups every day and to cut back on meat and oils."

28

HEALTHY CHOICES AHEAD

"My favorite part of the summer was teaching the kids about nutrition. They really seemed to enjoy learning about setting goals and making healthy decisions. I think that they're going to make great health advocates when they get back home," I said. "And if I ever open my own restaurant, I am going to make sure that the food is healthy and delicious!"

"I'm glad to hear that, Simon. I'll be your first customer! In the meantime, I hope you will be back at Whispering Pines Camp next summer. We make a great team," said Harold.

"I'll be back! You can count on it!" I said.

Just then, Ben came into the kitchen, holding a gold trophy. He was grinning widely as he said, "All right, I admit it, Simon! You won the bet! My tennis players were incredible yesterday! We beat Camp Silverbrook in the end of the summer tournament!"

"Congratulations, Ben! Harold and I can't take all the credit though. You coached them all summer. Good work." I then turned to Harold. "Have a great year, Harold. I'll see you next summer!"

Slim Goodbody Says: What have you discovered about making good food choices while reading this book? Make a mind map or a poster that shows what you have learned about nutrition from Simon and his friends. That way, you can share your knowledge with your friends and family!

GLOSSARY

arteries Tube-shaped vessels that carry blood away from the heart

calories Units of energy that are contained in foods and drinks. Calories are used to produce energy. Extra calories that are not used as energy may be stored as fat.

cartilage A strong, flexible material that makes up parts of the body, including the ears and nose

cholesterol A fatty substance that is found in food products that come from animals, such as milk, eggs, and meats. Too much cholesterol in the blood can build up on the walls of arteries and reduce blood flow, increasing your chances of having a heart attack or stroke

diabetes A disease in which a person has too much sugar in his or her blood. A person with diabetes cannot produce enough insulin, the substance that the body needs to use sugar properly

digest To break down food into the energy that the body needs to function

falafel Ground chickpeas and fava beans mixed with spices and fried

fiber Material in food that cannot be digested but helps with going to the bathroom

gender The sex of a person

high blood pressure A condition that forces the heart to work harder to pump blood

hummus A dip that is made with ground chickpeas, sesame-seed paste, lemon, and garlic

hydrogenated Describes a liquid fat that has been chemically altered into a solid fat, such as butter or margarine

infections Sicknesses or diseases caused by germs

nutrients Chemical compounds (such as protein, fat, carbohydrates, vitamins, or minerals) that make up foods. The body uses nutrients to function and grow

nutrition The study of food and diet

nutritious Describing foods that give the body energy and help it grow and heal

refined Describing a food that has had its nutritious parts removed

tissue A group or layer of cells that work together to perform a specific job in the body

valid Based on facts or evidence

FOR MORE INFORMATION

BAM Body and Mind Website by the Center for Disease Control
www.bam.gov/sub_foodnutrition/index.html
Learn interesting facts and play games about nutrition and making healthy choices about the food that you eat.

United States Department of Agriculture: MyPyramid
www.mypyramid.gov
Learn general information about the Food Pyramid and create a plan that will help you eat well and stay healthy.

United States Department of Agriculture: My Pyramid Animated
www.mypyramid.gov/global_nav/media_animation.html
View a fun, animated explanation of the Food Pyramid and the different food groups.

United States Department of Agriculture: MyPyramid for Kids
www.mypyramid.gov/kids/
Click on links to find information of the Food Pyramid, track your own intake of food and play nutrition games.

The Vegetarian Resource Group
www.vrg.org/nutrition/adapyramid.htm
Check out this diagram to learn more about the vegetarian food pyramid.

INDEX

ABOUT THE AUTHOR

John Burstein (also known as Slim Goodbody) has been entertaining and educating children for over thirty years. His programs have been broadcast on CBS, PBS, Nickelodeon, USA, and Discovery. He has won numerous awards including the Parent's Choice Award and the President's Council's Fitness Leader Award. Currently, Mr. Burstein tours the country with his live multimedia show "Bodyology." For more information, please visit slimgoodbody.com